WORLD WAR II
MOMENTS IN HISTORY

Shirley Jordan

COVER-TO-COVER BOOKS

Perfection Learning®

About the Author

Shirley Jordan is a retired elementary school teacher and principal. Currently a lecturer in the teacher-training program at California State University, Fullerton, California, she sees exciting things happening in the world of social studies. Shirley loves to travel—with a preference for sites important to U.S. history.

She has had more than 50 travel articles published in recent years. It was through her travels that she became interested in "moments in history," those ironic and little-known stories that make one exclaim, "I didn't know that!" Such stories are woven throughout her books.

Cover and Book Design: Deborah Lea Bell

Illustration: Michael A. Aspengren p. 8
Alan Stanley p. 30

Image Credits: Art Today title page, pp. 4 (top), 5 (top), 10, 13 (bottom), 24, 25, 26, 29, 41, 44, 56; Corbis© Digital Stock pp. 4 (bottom), 5 (middle and bottom), 9, 11, 12, 13 (top), 14, 16, 20 (top), 21, 33, 38, 45, 46, 48, 49 (Hulton-Deutsch Collection), 50, 51, 54, 59, 60, 61 (Hulton-Deutsch Collection); Library of Congress pp. 6, 17, 22; National Archives pp. 18, 20 (bottom), 32 (Rommel: 208-PU-154E-13752, Patton: 242-GAP-181A-4)

Table of Contents

A Timeline: The Early Years

1939 In September, German **dictator** Adolf Hitler sends troops into Poland. Britain and France declare war on Germany.

1940 In April, Germany attacks Denmark and Norway.

In May, Germany **invades** Belgium, Luxembourg, and the Netherlands.

In June, Italy declares war on Britain and France. France **surrenders** to Germany.

In October, Italian troops invade Greece.

In November, the countries of Hungary and Romania join Germany and Italy to become part of the Axis nations.

1941

In March, Bulgaria joins the Axis.

In April, Germany invades Greece and Yugoslavia.

In June, the Axis nations stage a surprise invasion of Russia.

In December, after the Japanese attack on Pearl Harbor, Germany and Italy declare war on the United States.

The U.S. declares war on Japan, Germany, and Italy.

Guam surrenders to the Japanese.

Wake Island surrenders to the Japanese.

Franklin D. Roosevelt

Chapter 1

When It Wasn't America's War

It was a Saturday late in 1941. Twelve-year-old Nancy and her brother Bob, 15, walked toward the only movie house in their small town. Each carried a banged-up metal pan. Turning in old pots and pans was important for the war in Europe.

Things were changing in the world. America's friends, the British, needed help. The U.S. was not part of the war in Europe. But President Roosevelt had a program to help the nations Germany had invaded. He called his program "Lend-Lease."

Nancy didn't understand how Lend-Lease worked. But putting her mother's old pans in a box in front of the theater would supposedly help the British.

Bob said American factories would turn the pans into guns, planes, and tanks. The British would use the weapons to fight Hitler.

But America was at peace. And Saturdays were special. Saturday had always been movie day. Each week, two out of three Americans went to a movie. Tickets were 25 cents in the evenings.

But for the Saturday afternoon show, a ticket was only 10 cents.

Nancy and Bob always walked to the theater together. Then they would split up to sit with friends.

But before they bought a ticket, Nancy and Bob had to make an important stop. No food was sold in theaters. So the young people flocked to the candy store across the street.

Nancy and her friends studied the offerings in the big glass cases. Nancy spent 5 cents for a roll of Necco Wafers. Her friend Laura chose Milk Duds. She bought a pack of gum too.

"I'll share with you," Laura told Nancy. "But remember to save the foil wrappers. It has something to do with guns for England."

The darkness of the theater was special. It seemed like a magic-carpet ride to adventure. True, the on-screen adventures were make-believe. But Nancy and her friends were children of the Great Depression. So they didn't have money for real-life family travel.

Once inside the dark theater, a uniformed usher carrying a flashlight helped them find their seats. The Popeye cartoon was about to begin.

It ended. Nancy slid down in her seat. She looked away from the screen. The newsreel would be next. It would show scenes from

Europe. They made Nancy uncomfortable. The flash of big guns. The wail of the air-raid sirens. All those marching men and rolling tanks. Often, the screen showed German crowds. "Heil Hitler!" they shouted.

"This isn't our war," Nancy whispered to Laura. "And I don't want to think about it."

Laura leaned closer. "Neither do I! My father says he'll join the Navy if America goes to war. I don't want him to go away."

Oh, no. What would my dad do? Nancy wondered.

She sighed with relief when the screen showed a giant movie camera swinging into place. The words across it read—

> **"Paramount News.**
> **The Eyes and Ears of the World.**
> **The End."**

Next came the *serial*. That was a story told in chapters. They saw a little bit each week. Most serials lasted four or five weeks. That month it featured Flash Gordon. He had ray guns and rocket ships.

"What a silly story," hissed Laura. "As if a man could fly to the moon!"

Each week's chapter would end with the hero in danger. Moviegoers had to wait seven days to see what happened next.

The *B movie* followed. This was a short film that was gray, grainy, and cheap to film. Some of Hollywood's most popular stars had started their careers this way. American audiences expected two films—a feature

and a B—each time they bought a movie ticket. Everyone wanted two, or a *double bill*, for the price of one.

The B movie was a detective story. It lasted just an hour. Nancy and Laura could hardly wait for the feature film. It was *Strike Up the Band*. It starred Mickey Rooney and Judy Garland. The story was about high school students trying to get their band to a national contest.

"I like this movie," Nancy whispered to Laura. "It's a lot better than thinking about Hitler."

After four hours, Nancy and Bob and their friends came out of the theater. They blinked in the afternoon sunlight. The magical Saturday matinee was over. In a few minutes, they were on their way home.

"You know what?" Bob asked when he and Nancy were halfway home. "I'm not so sure this won't be America's war. I heard Dad talking about that last night."

Oh, no, thought Nancy. President Roosevelt promised it wouldn't happen.

Bob went on. "Building Lend-Lease weapons isn't going to be enough. Dad says Hitler is going to invade the British Isles."

"Well, I don't think so," said Nancy. "After all, Christmas is coming. Certainly no one would start a war before Christmas!"

Chapter 2

Pearl Harbor

December 7, 1941

It was a calm Sunday morning. Dawn broke over the Hawaiian Islands. Many islanders were eating breakfast. Some were getting dressed for church. Others were still asleep. Early risers ran or strolled along the sands of Waikiki Beach. No one knew about the Japanese ships less than 250 miles away.

Six huge Japanese aircraft carriers rested on the waters of the Pacific Ocean. Thirty warships guarded them. Months of planning and spying had brought Japan to this day.

An hour before dawn, the signal came. Engines started. Wheels rolled. From the carrier decks soared 183 Japanese bombers and fighter planes. One after another. The planes started on the 90-minute flight to the Hawaiian island of Oahu.

These aircraft were leading a surprise attack against Hawaii and the U.S. Navy. As the first formations disappeared, another 183 planes rolled onto the carrier decks. They would form the second attack wave.

Japan wanted to be the strongest power in eastern Asia and the Pacific. Its leaders needed oil and metals from Indochina and British Malaya. But the U.S. and Britain stood in their way.

Japanese spies had watched ships come and go from Pearl Harbor. They hoped the attack would destroy most of the United States Navy.

The first planes arrived over Oahu. Half of them left the formation. They headed for airfields on various parts of the island.

The rest flew to Pearl Harbor. In their cockpits were postcards. They showed the fine, wide harbor from the air. Spies, disguised as vacationers, had bought the cards in Hawaiian gift shops months earlier.

The torpedo planes went first. They had to fly low. They were not very fast. So, for them, surprise was important. They flew straight to "Battleship Row." Seven battleships of the American Pacific Fleet were

anchored there. Skimming only 50 feet above water, the planes dropped torpedoes.

Explosions were felt everywhere. Huge holes were blown in the American ships. And the ships began to sink. The Navy men were surprised. Few of them found their way to their gun stations on deck. Those who did fought bravely and shot well. A few Japanese planes

fell into the water.

After 20 minutes, the Japanese torpedo bombers flew away. They were replaced by high-altitude bombers. Behind those roared the Japanese dive-bombers. Explosions filled the air. Bombs crashed onto the ships. Piers and supply depots were flattened. Buildings and **hangars** on the shore exploded.

The worst loss of the day was

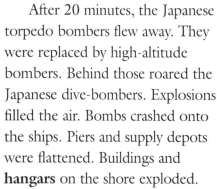

the battleship *Arizona*. Its bottom was ripped away by a torpedo. Then the ship was hit by eight Japanese bombs. Seconds later, the *Arizona's* gunpowder supply exploded. Flames shot more than 1,000 feet into the air. In less than ten minutes, it sank to the bottom of the harbor.

Many men were killed by the blast. Others were trapped below decks. They drowned. The total dead on the *Arizona* reached 1,177.

Meanwhile, the other 91 Japanese planes swooped down upon Oahu's five air bases. These were Wheeler Field, Bellows Field, Hickam Field, Ewa Field, and the Kaneohe Naval Air Station. Plane after plane was destroyed. One bomb struck a **barracks** building. It killed the 100 men sleeping inside.

The attack ended. It had lasted less than two hours. The Japanese pilots headed back to their aircraft carriers. The carriers were still waiting 250 miles out at sea. Behind the Japanese pilots left a scene of destruction and death.

At Pearl Harbor, three battleships were completely destroyed. They were the *Oklahoma,* the *Arizona,* and the *West Virginia*.

The *Nevada* had run aground. The *California* was sinking. The *Maryland,* the *Tennessee,* and the *Pennsylvania* were in bad condition.

But they could be repaired. Eleven other ships had been sunk.

Fortunately, America's two aircraft carriers had been out to sea. So they were not caught in the trap.

At the airfields, 188 American planes had been burned. Another 160 were damaged. Hangars and control towers were gone.

The worst news was the loss of life. Counting civilians caught in the attack, 2,403 Americans died that Sunday morning. Almost half of those died on one ship, the *Arizona*.

Was the attack upon Pearl Harbor a complete surprise? Almost.

President Roosevelt had suspected a Japanese attack. Somewhere in the Pacific. The government reasoned that it would be in the area of British Malaya.

But such an attack seemed far off. Especially since Japanese representatives were in Washington, D.C., that very day. They were pretending to talk about peace.

Pearl Harbor
A Deadly Surprise

U.S. Casualties

Navy	2,008 killed	710 wounded
Marines	109 killed	69 wounded
Army	218 killed	364 wounded
Civilian	68 killed	35 wounded

Japanese Casualties

64 killed (plus an unknown number of crew members aboard the large submarine)

U.S. Ships and Aircraft Damaged or Destroyed

battleship *Arizona*
battleship *California*
battleship *Maryland*
battleship *Nevada*
battleship *Oklahoma*
battleship *Pennsylvania*
battleship *Tennessee*
battleship *West Virginia*
cruiser *Helena*
cruiser *Honolulu*
cruiser *Raleigh*
destroyer *Cassin*
destroyer *Downes*
destroyer *Shaw*
minelayer *Oglala*
repair ship *Vestal*
seaplane tender *Curtiss*
target ship *Utah*
224 Army planes
123 Navy planes

Japanese Ships and Aircraft Destroyed

29 planes
One large submarine
Five two-man subs

Could the attack have been detected? Well, it was! At about 7 o'clock that morning, an Army radar screen on Oahu showed a number of blips. At that time, the Japanese planes were still more than 100 miles from Hawaii.

The two servicemen stationed there called a lieutenant. They reported what they saw. The lieutenant decided the blips were probably caused by some U.S. bombers. The bombers were to arrive that day from California. And nothing more was done to investigate.

One part of the enemy attack was unsuccessful. Six Japanese midget submarines were cruising just off the coast of Oahu. It was their job to sneak into Pearl Harbor. They were supposed to add to the confusion and destruction. But U.S. warships discovered them. The small subs quickly moved away.

Interestingly, the first vessel lost at Pearl Harbor was a full-sized Japanese submarine. It was lurking outside the harbor. Fifteen minutes before the attack, a U.S. destroyer spotted it. The destroyer sank the sub with gunfire and **depth charges.**

Another Japanese submarine in those waters ran aground that day. Its commander was arrested. He became the first prisoner taken by the Americans in World War II.

Chapter 3

America
Gets Involved

After Pearl Harbor, life changed for Nancy, Bob, and their friends. Everyone was afraid of enemy attacks.

Eastern citizens feared the Germans would arrive in destroyers and battleships. People near the Great Lakes had nightmares about a submarine attack. In California, Oregon, and Washington, people expected an all-out Japanese invasion.

Thousands of men enlisted in the armed forces. Millions of others were **drafted** into service. As the men left for training, women filled their places at work.

Some worked in war plants. Others replaced men in offices.

A 60-hour workweek was common. Often, factories ran on *shifts*. They had three eight-hour work periods each day. The machinery ran without stopping.

Air-raid drills were held. Families practiced what to do in case of an air attack. School hallways held buckets of sand to put out fires. After dark, the windows of homes were shaded. Streetlights were set low. And cars drove with only their parking lights.

Americans helped the war effort by staying close to home. Gas was scarce. It went to military trucks, jeeps, and tanks first. No new cars were built.

Young people, like Nancy and Bob, did their part. They planted "victory gardens" with rows of vegetables and fruits. In 1943, these gardens produced one-third of all the vegetables eaten in the U.S.

To help the government pay for the war effort, children bought war stamps. This was a way for them to lend money to their country.

BUY WAR BONDS

The stamps could be pasted in a booklet and saved until after the war. Then the young people could cash them in and get their money back.

Children's savings stamps earned no interest. But their parents could buy *savings bonds*. These increased in value. The cheapest war bond cost $18.75. If kept for ten years, it could be cashed for $25.00. An investment of $37.50 grew to become a $50.00 bond. And $75.00 would later be worth $100.00.

Few Americans could afford to buy larger bonds. It was too soon after the Depression.

Supplying the Army, Navy, and Marines required huge truckloads of food and clothing. So civilians had to wait. Meat, fish, sugar, coffee, canned goods, and dairy products were scarce. Especially butter!

To share these items fairly, the government gave books of ration stamps to each American. To buy something, the shopper had to turn over the money and the proper number of stamps.

Two pounds a week per person was the meat allowance. Most people observed "meatless Tuesday." Shoe purchases were limited to two pairs per person, per year.

Japan had seized most of the Asian areas that produced rubber. With all the military trucks and jeeps in service, tires were difficult to find at home. The government began rationing gasoline. This helped save gas. And it cut down on tire wear.

Each car had a sticker in the window. The sticker had a letter on it—A through E. Most Americans had an A sticker. That meant they could buy three gallons of gas a week. To get more, a worker had to prove it was needed for his job. A doctor who made house calls or a minister visiting the sick might have an E sticker.

Nylon was still very new in 1941. Most women's stockings had been made of silk. When both silk and nylon were needed for parachutes, stockings became very hard to find.

As a result, women began to paint their legs. The light brown mixture they used was similar to finger paint. Few women ever became good at rubbing it on evenly. No matter how hard they tried!

Homes didn't have television in 1941. But radio programs joined the war effort. Some programs, such as *Terry and the Pirates,* told of enemy action in the Pacific. The program's hero usually performed dramatic rescues.

At the movies, cartoon characters like Donald Duck and Bugs Bunny collected scrap metal. They planted victory gardens too.

Comic book heroes fought the Germans and the Japanese. Captain

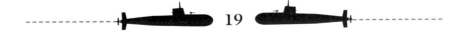

Marvel went after the evil Dr. Savannah. The doctor worked for German agents.

Superman fought spies too. But he surprised his readers. He failed his Army physical exam. His X-ray vision melted the machine used to check his eyes!

Girls like Nancy knitted woolen squares to make blankets for the wounded. Boys found other interests. Most could tell a Mustang fighter plane from a Thunderbolt. They knew the outlines of the B-17 bomber and the B-24.

Pictures of American planes plastered the walls of boys' bedrooms. Through it all, they wondered whether the war would last long enough to include them.

The draft age dropped to 18. Now it really was their war.

Chapter

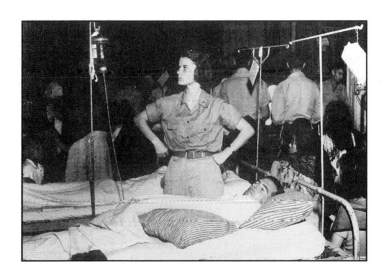

American Women in Uniform

Ever since the Revolution, American women had helped their country during wartime. They had fought alongside their husbands on the battlefield. And they had nursed wounded soldiers. Many women had served in World War I—most of them as typists. Now thousands of women were again eager to help.

Congress was slow to agree to military service for women.

A Michigan representative named Hoffman asked—

"If you take women into the armed services, then who will do the cooking, the washing, the mending, the humble, homey tasks to which every woman has devoted herself?"

The debates went on for weeks. Congress slowly began to accept the idea of women leaving their homes for the war effort. But only unmarried women would be allowed.

The WASP

More than 1,000 women served in the Women's Air Force Service Pilots. Most had learned to fly before the war. They had the important role of flying airplanes between military bases. They also delivered cargo. And they tested new planes. Their work freed up men to fly in combat.

The WAAC

The Women's Army Auxiliary Corps was formed. The "WAACs," as they were called, trained for six weeks. Then the women worked in military offices all over the nation. This allowed thousands more men to enter combat. About 80,000 women served the WAAC during the war. Many were sent overseas.

The WAVES

The Navy also started a women's corps. It was called the Women Accepted for Voluntary Emergency Service. Like the WAAC, the WAVES had high standards. Women had to have a college degree. Or two years of college and two years of work experience. The women of the WAVES received the same wages and benefits as Navy men. This was not true of the other women's services.

The SPARS and the MCWR

The U.S. Coast Guard and the U.S. Marine Corps also formed groups for women. The name SPARS was taken from the Coast Guard's Latin motto. This group hoped to enroll 1,000 officers and 10,000 enlisted women.

The Marine Corps Women's Reserve was open to 1,000 officers and 18,000 enlisted women.

Unlike those in the Army, women in the Navy, Coast Guard, and Marines were not sent overseas.

The Nurses

During World War II, 60,000 women belonged to the Army Nurse Corps. They served all over the world. Often, they were on the front lines of battle. In the Pacific, dozens were captured by the Japanese. They were held as prisoners. More than 200 nurses were killed in World War II. And 1,600 nurses earned medals.

In the closing years of the war, women had proven their value to the military. Soon they were given jobs formerly held only by men. Some received training in military intelligence, communications, and supply operations. Others were aerial photographers, radio operators, weather forecasters, and control tower operators.

Chapter 5

The Leaders of War

The Allied Nations

Between 1939 and 1945, 46 countries joined the U.S., England, and Russia to support the Allied cause.

Franklin Delano Roosevelt

became U.S. president in 1932. He was crippled by polio. And he governed from a wheelchair. He steered the nation out of the Great Depression.

A strong speaker and leader, he was very popular. Americans trusted him to lead them to peace. And they elected him as their president four times. Roosevelt died just a few weeks before the Nazis were defeated.

Winston Churchill became the British prime minister in 1940. His stirring speeches helped the English hold on to hope.

He and Roosevelt developed a strong friendship. Churchill knew the war was hopeless without Russia's military forces. But he never trusted Joseph Stalin as an **ally.**

Joseph Stalin was a cruel dictator of Russia. He was a one-time supporter of Hitler. Nazi troops invaded Russia in 1941. Stalin was surprised. He asked for guns and planes from England and America.

In 1942 and 1943, he begged the Allies to attack the Nazis on the west coast of France. But Churchill and Roosevelt needed time to prepare. The attack, called D-Day, came on June 6, 1944.

The Axis Nations

Seven nations formed the Axis nations: Germany, Italy, Japan, Bulgaria, Finland, Hungary, and Romania.

Adolf Hitler served in the German army in World War I. He blamed the Jews and Communists for the loss of that war. He said that they "stabbed Germany in the back."

Hitler formed the Nazi Party in 1933. He was elected **chancellor** of Germany. Later, he became its dictator.

In 1939, Hitler's troops moved to grab land from Poland and all of western Europe. He attacked Russia. And he tried to invade Britain. The world came to know him as a madman with a vast army afraid to resist him.

Benito Mussolini was Italy's dictator for 21 years. He controlled his people with threats of murder and imprisonment. After the Germans had almost beaten the French in 1940, Mussolini entered World War II. He invaded southern France. In 1943, the Italians tried to throw him out. But German parachute troops saved him.

Emperor Hirohito of Japan wanted more land for his country. He allowed his military leaders to take territory from other nations. In 1931, Japan invaded China. Then ten years later on December 7, 1941, Japan attacked Pearl Harbor. They took over most of the American, British, and Dutch Islands in the Pacific Ocean.

In 1945, Hirohito saw that Japan would be defeated. He refused to give up. Unless he could remain emperor. President Truman agreed, as long as the Japanese people voted for him in a free election. The new constitution of Japan in 1947 made him a democratic monarch.

Chapter 6

Attacks upon American Soil

Europe, Africa, and parts of Asia were torn apart by the war. Luckily, the U.S. mainland suffered very little damage. But here are a few times that the Japanese slipped through U.S. West Coast defenses.

Monterey, California

On December 20, 1941, some Northern Californians got a big surprise. It had been less than two weeks since Pearl Harbor. An American tanker was sailing through Pacific waters. It was near Monterey's beautiful Cypress Point Golf Course. It was Saturday morning. Citizens strolled along the shoreline. Golfers dotted the fairways overlooking the ocean.

The tanker, the *Agwiworld,* was not armed. No one expected danger so close to the rolling green hills of Cypress Point.

Suddenly, a Japanese submarine broke through the water. Shocked Californians watched as it attacked the *Agwiworld.* Some of the people ran away. Others hid behind trees.

The ship's captain, Frederico Borges Goncalves, had fought in

World War I. He knew a lot about submarines.

"The first thing I knew," he said later, "a **shell** exploded over our stern. I was in my cabin. And I ran to the bridge. Right away, I had our radioman send a message to the Navy and all other ships."

The submarine lay 500 yards west of the tanker. "I put the helm hard to port and turned the ship straight for the sub," Goncalves said. "The sub was firing again. She fired four shots that came very close and splashed water over our bow."

The sea was rough that morning. There was a great deal of wind. This was good fortune for the tanker. For it was difficult for the Japanese to aim their gun.

Five or six men slid about on the deck of the submarine. Captain Goncalves watched through his binoculars. If the sub speeded up, the men at the gun might be swept overboard.

The tanker's bow was moving straight for the submarine. Captain Goncalves ordered, "Full speed ahead!" His unarmed ship would do battle the only way it could. By ramming the sub.

Quickly, the Japanese commander moved his vessel out of the way. In moments, the sub had disappeared underwater.

The tanker had missed its chance to ram the submarine. So it turned and headed for the safety of Monterey Bay. Moving at full speed, the *Agwiworld* disappeared in a blanket of her own smoke.

Those watching from the Cypress Point shore were frightened. But they laughed at what the men on the *Agwiworld* did next. Excited at having driven the enemy away, the sailors crowded around the rail. They cursed their bad luck at having no weapons, though. So they threw raw potatoes at the spot where the sub had disappeared.

Fort Stevens, Oregon

Oregon and Washington took a leading role in U.S. military shipbuilding during the war. So there was much concern that enemy attacks might occur along their coasts.

On June 21, 1942, a Japanese submarine surfaced near Oregon's Fort Stevens. Before the Americans could respond, the sub launched a series of 17 shells.

The Japanese were far from shore and out of reach of the fort's guns. The men of Fort Stevens waited to defend their position. But the submarine turned and headed out to sea. None of the Japanese shells had damaged the fort.

This was the only U.S. mainland military post that had been fired upon since the War of 1812.

Brookings, Oregon

On September 9, 1942, an enemy submarine surfaced off the coast of southern Oregon. It carried a crew of 100. And it had a Japanese pilot, Nobuo Fujita. It also brought with it a small seaplane with folded wings.

In the early morning darkness, the crew put the plane together. And they straightened its wings. Then they shot it into the air, using a *catapult*. That's an instrument like a giant slingshot.

Fujita used a lighthouse at Cape Bianco as his guide. He adjusted the controls. And he flew over the mountains. There he dropped two 168-pound firebombs onto the wooded slopes. The Japanese hoped to start huge forest fires.

Some hunters had spotted Fujita's plane. And they had sent a warning to the military. Meanwhile, the hunters used the only weapons they had to fire at the plane—their deer rifles.

The pilot flew back to the submarine. He landed near it, using his plane's **pontoons.** The crew hurried to stow the small plane. Then they dove to 250 feet and waited quietly.

The Navy arrived and dropped depth charges. But they did not find the enemy.

Twenty days later, Fujita repeated the mission. This time, he flew in the dark. Because of the heavy rains and green forests of Oregon, only one of the bombs caused a fire. It was quickly put out by forest rangers.

Fujita's flights pleased his leaders in Japan. But he later felt ashamed about what he had done.

Twenty years passed. In 1962, the people of Brookings invited their former enemy to visit the town. Fujita was surprised about the invitation. But he was glad. Now he could apologize.

But he wondered how he would be received. Would the people of Oregon be angry with him? Just in case, he brought along a valuable 400-year-old Samurai sword. If the citizens of Brookings were angry, Fujita planned to use the sword to kill himself.

When he arrived, he was treated with great respect. So the Samurai sword became a fine gift for the town. Later,

Fujita gave $1,000 to the Brookings library to buy books about Japan for children. So there wouldn't be another war between Japan and the United States.

The Bly Church Picnic

Throughout the war, Japan released thousands of balloons carrying bombs. The winds carried them over the Pacific to the western U.S. Some of them set fires. Only one of those bombs took American lives.

The Bly Church was near Brookings, Oregon. (The same area that Fujita had bombed.) In May 1945, the church held its annual picnic. The picnic spot—Salt Springs—was crowded. Families played games and filled their plates with chicken and potato salad.

Suddenly, a gust of wind brought a balloon soaring into the crowd. Hanging from it was a large bomb. There was a fiery explosion. And six people lay dead. These are the only recorded deaths from wartime attacks upon the United States mainland.

A Timeline: The War Continues in Europe

1942

In June, the U.S. declares war on Bulgaria, Hungary, and Romania.

German troops seize Tobruk in North Africa.

In September, German troops enter Stalingrad, Russia.

In November, Allied forces land in North Africa.

1943

In February, Russia retakes Stalingrad.

In May, the Allies take key areas of Africa. Most German forces in Africa are beaten.

In July, Allied forces invade the Italian island of Sicily.

In September, the Allies invade Italy.

In October, Italian dictator Mussolini is forced out.

Italy declares war on Germany.

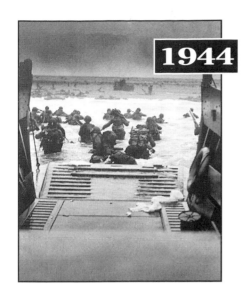

1944

In January, the Russians drive the Germans out of Leningrad.

The Allies land in Normandy, France, on D-Day in June.

The first German V-1 rocket lands on London.

Romania declares war on Germany.

In September, Bulgaria declares war on Germany.

In December, the Allies fight to drive the Germans back at the Battle of the Bulge.

1945

Russian troops drive the Germans back into Poland and take Warsaw.

Hungary declares war on Germany.

The Russians reach the **suburbs** of Berlin, Germany's capital.

After many months of fighting, the Germans from both east and west, the U.S., and Russian troops meet.

In May, German troops in Italy surrender. Germany surrenders to the Allies on May 7, 1945.

Chapter 7

Choosing a Day for Battle

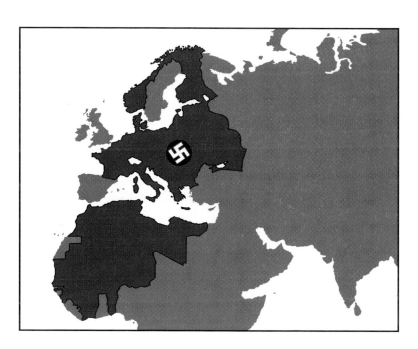

In September 1942, Germany and Italy held Europe in their grip. The lands they occupied stretched from Norway to North Africa. And from France to western Russia.

The British Isles were fighting to keep the Germans out. They needed supplies that had to pass through the Mediterranean Sea. But the Axis held the shores of southern Europe and northern Africa. America was not yet strong enough to invade Hitler in Europe. But the Americans and the British hoped to loosen the Nazi hold on North Africa.

Jerome Namias paced the floor. How could he make such an important decision? What if his information was wrong? How many Americans might die in battle because of his mistake?

Namias was a respected scientist. He was a pioneer in weather-forecasting. He had found ways to predict what the weather would be days, even weeks, ahead.

As a boy, Namias had been a good student. But not an outstanding one. School was easy for him. So he often didn't try as hard as he should have. This all changed when he was in college.

One day, Namias began to feel sick and very weak. A doctor examined him. He said Namias had *tuberculosis*. This was a serious disease of the lungs. And it called for months of bed rest. It was the only treatment known then. Namias was forced to drop out of college.

Now he had lots of time. There wasn't much the doctor would let him do. So he began to read. He studied physics and astronomy. And he taught himself to speak German. He was particularly fascinated with *meteorology*. That's the study of the weather.

Namias read about air masses, wind direction, and pressure systems. He studied the almanacs of Benjamin Franklin and Benjamin Banneker. These men had truly led the way in weather prediction.

After long months in bed, he was cured of tuberculosis. He finished college. Then he earned a master's degree and began to teach high school physics.

All the while, Namias continued to study meteorology. Finally, his studies were recognized. He was hired at the United States National

Weather Service. It was in Washington, D.C.

Before the war, that office answered such questions as—

"What will the weather be like for graduation at Harvard University?"

"Will it snow on Inauguration Day?"

The questions were never a matter of life or death.

Namias continued to find improved ways of gathering information. He grew better at predicting the weather. At the beginning of World War II, he was director of the U.S. Weather Bureau.

Now it was November 1942. Namias faced his most important assignment.

The Allies had secret plans to invade North Africa in three places along the coast. They needed to push the Germans and Italians back. So supplies for the Allies could again travel through the Mediterranean Sea.

The attack was called "Operation Torch." Much of its success depended upon choosing the right date. That was Jerome Namias's job.

Namias was ordered to keep Operation Torch a secret. He could not talk to his coworkers or his family about it. And he could not use the **telegraph** to get information from European weather stations. The Germans would guess why he was asking.

Radar was new in 1942. It was being tested to track aircraft. But it could not yet predict weather. **Satellite** weather stations were a far-off dream.

Namias studied his charts and graphs. He checked all the figures again. At home, he paced the floor for hours. Finally, he met with the military leaders.

"November 7 and 8," he said. "That's the best time for Operation Torch."

The weather was clear. And the Allies were ready. Operation Torch was a success. In fact, it marked the turning point of World War II. The Allies were on the road to victory.

Chapter

Tricking the Germans

As 1943 ended, the Nazis still controlled most of Europe. The Germans had occupied France for four years.

The British were weak from months of bombing. The Russians were fighting to drive the Nazis back from their land. If the Allies were to defeat Hitler, they would have to invade Europe through France. Only then could they get to Berlin, Germany's capital.

The Allies gathered in the south of Britain. Hitler's army waited just 25 miles away. They were on the other side of the English Channel.

In November 1943, President Roosevelt went to Iran. He met with British Prime Minister Winston Churchill. And with Russia's Premier Joseph Stalin. These three Allied leaders needed a plan. They agreed to call the plan "Operation Overlord."

The attack would begin on a date called "D-Day." American and British forces would lead the attack. Russia's troops would fight hard to save their own country and keep the Germans busy. The Allied leaders appointed American General Dwight D. Eisenhower to lead the invasion.

First, the Allies had to break through Hitler's "Atlantic Wall." It was not really a wall. It was a wide row of mines, forts, heavy guns, and machine-gun nests. This row of defenses stretched 50 miles. It formed a line just inside the beaches of western France.

For nearly a year, the Germans had marked a large map. It showed the most likely spots for an Allied invasion. As spies sent in reports, Hitler studied the possibilities. His eyes raced around the map. One day, he expected an attack in Norway or in Holland. Then the next day, he thought Normandy or Brittany in France would be attacked. Sometimes he thought troops would land in Portugal or Spain.

Roosevelt, Churchill, and Eisenhower knew an invasion would be difficult. And many men in the Allied forces would die. But part of a good military plan was surprise. Perhaps there were ways to trick the Germans.

Secrecy would not be easy. Nearly 3 million men would take part in D-Day. These troops would need 6,000 vessels of many kinds. This would mean bringing together ships, trucks, guns, and ammunition in huge numbers.

There was no way to keep the Germans from knowing about such a buildup of forces. Certainly, there were spies on English soil. And the

Germans flew regular information-gathering, or *reconnaissance,* flights. Their planes passed over the English Channel to photograph what the British were doing.

Finally, the Allies agreed on a plan. On D-Day, a huge fleet of bombers would fly over the French coast. It would happen at 3:00 A.M. They would drop bombs on Hitler's Atlantic Wall.

Then at dawn, a few thousand Allied men would lead the attack on the beaches. Gliders would pass above. They would drop hundreds of **paratroopers** into the villages beyond the wall.

Once the beaches were clear, wave after wave of Allies would follow. These troops would float tanks and huge guns across the channel on **barges.**

The weather had to be just right. A British meteorologist was chosen to advise the Allies. He told General Eisenhower that the best combination of moon, clouds, and tide would come on June 5, 6, and 7. Moonlight was needed so the attacking forces could see the French shoreline. And there should be very few clouds.

The tide was the most important. It had to be high enough to allow landing craft filled with men to float over the Germans' concrete and wooden barriers.

After the first Allied troops had landed, there had to be a second high tide that same day. Daylight and deep water would be needed for the landing of tanks and guns.

The attack could not be held before June. Because not all the landing craft had been delivered to the south of England.

But waiting until after June was dangerous. Hitler was very close to having a powerful new weapon. His scientists were working on a rocket designed to soar over the English Channel. It would explode on British soil with great force.

General Eisenhower gathered all the reports. Choosing D-Day was his job. He decided on June 6, 1944. The attack would be at a region of France called Normandy.

Five major assaults would strike the French coast. The Americans

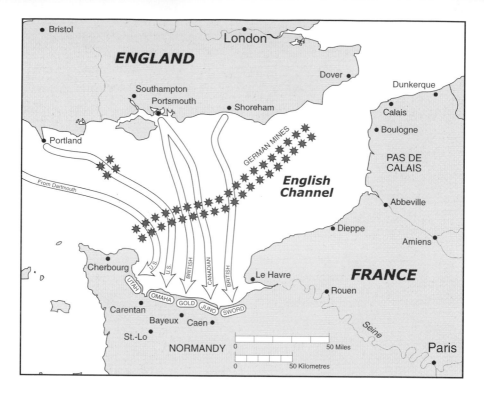

Bristol
ENGLAND
London
Dover
Dunkerque
Southampton
Portsmouth
Shoreham
Calais
Boulogne
Portland
GERMAN MINES
PAS DE CALAIS
From Dartmouth
English Channel
Abbeville
Amiens
Dieppe
Cherbourg
US
US
BRITISH
CANADIAN
BRITISH
Le Havre
FRANCE
Rouen
Carentan
UTAH
OMAHA
GOLD
JUNO
SWORD
Bayeux
Caen
St.-Lo
NORMANDY
Seine
Paris
0   50 Miles
0   50 Kilometres

would attack beaches code-named Omaha and Utah. The British, Canadians, and other Allied troops would land at other areas of Normandy. They were called Sword, Juno, and Gold.

The British and American spy offices worked together. It was likely that Hitler would expect an attack somewhere along the French beaches. The shortest distance across the English Channel was 25 miles. That was between the ports of Dover, England, and Calais, France.

The Allies wanted Hitler to believe the attack would come at Calais. How could they trick him?

Eisenhower and his advisors chose Normandy for a reason. The distance across the English Channel would be three times as far. But the extra distance was worth it to fool the enemy. The British and Americans "helped" the Nazis turn their attention to Calais.

They tricked the Germans about who would be the commander of D-Day. General George Patton was one of America's smartest officers. But his temper made some worry about his leadership abilities.

Patton had played a key role in Allied victories in North Africa,

Sicily, and Italy. But he had shocked the American people. He had slapped a wounded soldier and called him a coward.

President Roosevelt refused to consider Patton as the D-Day leader. But what if the Germans thought he was in charge? Might they use their spies in the wrong places?

To set a trap for the enemy, Patton would seem to be the commander. A make-believe First U.S. Army Group (FUSAG) was invented. It was supposedly made up of 50 divisions. That's 1 million men!

The Americans leaked news reports that FUSAG was training near Dover. Now the Nazis were certain. Patton and this huge army would strike at Calais. So they stationed their finest fighting force—the 15th Army—along that beach.

English movie studios built phony landing craft. They anchored them in the Thames River. (It flows through London to the sea.) At Dover, a fake oil dock covered three square miles. A make-believe military base and army hospital were added nearby.

At a secret location called Camp X, near Toronto, Canada, more tricks were in the works. Jasper Maskelyne, a magician, invented a rubber material. It was used for shapes that could be filled with air.

Soon Camp X had produced 400 such shapes. They were made to look like tanks, trucks, and huge guns. By May, these had been shipped to Dover. They were inflated and placed around the countryside. As they looked down, **reconnaissance** pilots from Germany thought they saw huge buildups of equipment.

These shapes were easy to move about. Every night, men carried the fake trucks and jeeps to different positions. The Germans never caught on.

Allied agents used rumors, false telegrams, and secret agents. These helped keep the Nazis confused.

"Project Fortitude," another plan, was designed to keep Nazi troops as far from Normandy as possible. The Allies sent out false hints over the radio. German spies believed that a 250,000-man "British 4th Army" was gathering in Scotland. They were fooled by radio messages. The messages talked about "ski training" and "climbing rock faces."

The confused Germans were sure an Allied strike was coming to snow-covered Norway. There really was no British 4th Army. But the trick worked. The Germans moved 17 army divisions to Norway. That was a total of 340,000 men!

An extra bit of luck came to the Allies. General Erwin Rommel was a German hero and very strict leader. He was in charge of the troops along the Atlantic Wall. He had been called to Berlin for a one-day meeting. It was his wife's birthday. So Rommel extended his trip for an extra day at his German home in Stuttgart.

The Atlantic Wall was left without a strong leader. And the German troops were not sure how to proceed when the attack came. So there was a delay. It was at least a day before German land forces headed for the Normandy beaches.

D-Day was a success. The shores of Normandy became Allied territory. But the victory was a difficult one. Day by day, mile by mile, the troops moved forward. From those first five beaches, they pushed their way through France and then Germany.

Thousands of troops died on D-Day and in the following 11 months. But without the American and British spy teams, the losses might have been far higher.

Chapter

A Soldier's Journal

The Horror of the Death Camps

Adolf Hitler made it clear he wanted to be rid of what he called the "diseased" races. He wished to destroy all of Europe's Jews, gypsies, the mentally ill, and the physically handicapped.

During World War II, the Germans killed between 10 and 12 million prisoners. More than 6 million of them were Jewish.

In the U.S., citizens had heard only hints about Europe's **death camps.** Many Jews had fled to America from 1936 to 1939. But even they knew little of what had happened to the loved ones they'd left behind. After the war, the world learned of the great evil known as the Holocaust.

Here is a U.S. army lieutenant's journal. Share a few days with him at Bergen-Belsen. It was the first German prison camp freed by the Allies.

April 15, 1945

We were 200 yards from Bergen-Belsen this morning. That's when the smell reached us. Death has been with us every day on the battlefield. But this was different. We knew what lay ahead was the smell of suffering. And these were not soldiers. These were the innocent.

We broke through the gate with our trucks. But it didn't matter. The Nazi guards had all run away. What we found were crowds of skeletonlike prisoners. They were dying.

Some tried to come toward us. They were stumbling and crawling and reaching out.

Most were too weak to move forward. But they turned their sunken-cheeked faces to us. Glassy eyes, filled with tears, turned our way. Some of my own men, even the toughest in battle, wiped away tears.

We will never forget the sight. Piled against the back fence are 3,000 stick-thin dead bodies. The Germans had not yet buried or burned them.

A crew has begun work there. They will write down the numbers tattooed by the Germans on each prisoner's arm. Perhaps that will help with identification.

April 16, 1945

The Army Nurses and the American Red Cross must have worked all night. Now those of the 40,000 starving, sick prisoners who had no blankets are covered. Prisoners who can feed themselves seem stronger already. Everyone is busy spooning food into the very weakest men. Soon everyone will have had a shower or sponge bath.

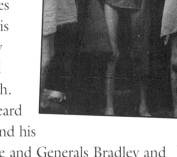

General "Ike" Eisenhower heard about what we found here. Ike and his men are just a few miles away. He and Generals Bradley and Patton will be here tomorrow.

Twenty-six of the freed prisoners died during the night. We arrived too late for them.

April 17, 1945

I can see why G.I.s talk about General Eisenhower and his leadership. The three generals came early today. Ike and his old friend, General Omar Bradley, spent hours talking to the camp prisoners. Some had been locked up at two or more camps. They told of riding on trains for days. They had been jammed into cattle cars.

They told of camps where gas chambers killed hundreds. Of air filled with the smell of burning bodies. Some said their children had been ripped away from them and never seen again.

The horror here was too much for General "Blood and Guts" Patton. My men say he went over to a nearby **latrine** and vomited. Who can blame him?

Eisenhower spoke to us before he left. He said, "I want every

American unit not actually at the front to see this place. Now [each soldier] will at least know what he is fighting against."

Another 30 of Bergen-Belsen's weakest died last night.

April 18, 1945

Other troops came through today. Many couldn't stomach it. A lot of men brought candy bars. It's not the kind of food the former prisoners need now. But I guess the G.I.s just wanted to do something—anything.

General Eisenhower had an even better idea. Today, our men paraded the German people from the town through here. It's time they had a look.

Some of the townspeople just looked stone-faced. Many refused to look at the bodies. And most of them cried. They shook their heads. I don't speak German. But I think they were saying they hadn't known what went on here. Can we believe them?

My unit must push on tomorrow. We'll be entering many more of these camps. I just hope the world never forgets what happened here.

I know I never will.

Chapter 10

Children in Hiding

Europe's Jews lived in terror. The horrors of Hitler's policies closed in around them. Six million of them—men, women, children, and babies—would die in the Holocaust.

But there was another group of Jewish children. These were the hundreds of children in hiding. Given up by their terrified parents, they left their homes and towns. And they hid to stay alive.

The secret lives of these children took many forms. A few, who did not look Jewish, remained in sight. They took Christian names. They learned to lie about their families and where they had come from.

The kind non-Jews who took these children in treated them like part of the family. They risked their own lives. They lied to neighbors. They said they were caring for a young orphaned niece or nephew.

However, most of the hidden children were forced to drop out of sight. They were hidden in Catholic **convents** or in orphanages. They, too, were taught to lie about their names and homes.

Even the other children at the orphanages could not know the truth. Sometimes, Nazis searched the convents and orphanages. They looked for hidden Jews. So the fewer people who could give away the secret, the better.

In some ways, the children in the orphanages were lucky. They had other boys and girls to play with. They had a place to sleep and enough to eat.

Worse off were the children hidden in haylofts, attics, and basements. They had to remain silent. They were alone and friendless. They spent long hours peeking out from behind curtains. They could see other children at play. And people who could tell on them were all around.

These hidden children were robbed of their childhood. They were sick with worry. Were their parents still alive? Or had they been taken to the death camps? If their parents lived, how would they find each other after the war?

When the war ended, four years had passed. The Allies opened the death camps. The few survivors hurried to claim their

hidden children. But in far too many cases, the parents had been murdered by the Nazis. Or they had been worked to death in slave camps.

Many children remained in the orphanages. Others relied on the Red Cross to help find relatives there in Europe.

Teenage children, now orphans, wandered the roads of Europe. They were searching for new homes. And new lives. Many lived in camps set up for displaced persons. From there, they moved to whatever country would take them.

The stress from years of hiding caused many to lapse into mental illness. Some committed suicide.

The lucky ones were able to make new lives. Many left Europe. They went to live with relatives in Israel or the United States.

Grateful to be alive, most of the hidden children worked hard. They took any jobs they could get. They had missed years of schooling. But many aimed high in their education.

Today, the hidden children have become educators, doctors, and scientists. Many have won honors and medals.

It was years before most of them came forward with their war stories. They felt guilty. Why? Because they had lived. While so many others had died.

Now these survivors are in their sixties and seventies. And they all agree—

It is their wish that all children of the world live in freedom. There must be no more reason to hide.

A Timeline: The War Continues in the Pacific

1942

Japanese capture the Philippine Islands from the U.S.

Japanese troops land in the Dutch East Indies.

In February, Singapore surrenders to the Japanese.

The Allies lose the Battle of the Java Sea.

In April, U.S. troops on Bataan surrender to the Japanese.

In May, the Allies win the Battle of the Coral Sea. This saves Australia from invasion.

The Japanese take over Corregidor.

In June, the Battle of Midway stops Japan's move eastward across the Pacific.

In August, U.S. Marines land on Guadalcanal.

1943

In March, U.S. warships defeat the Japanese in the Battle of the Bismarck Sea.

In May, the Japanese give up trying to invade the Aleutian Islands of Alaska.

In November, U.S. troops land on the islands of Bougainville, Tarawa, and Makin.

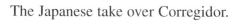

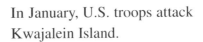
1944

In January, U.S. troops attack Kwajalein Island.

In February, U.S. naval forces raid Truk Island.

Allied soldiers land in the Admiralty Islands.

In June, U.S. forces invade Saipan Island.

The U.S. sends B-29 bombers to raid Japan.

U.S. forces win the Battle of the Philippine Sea.

In July, U.S. troops land on Guam Island.

In October, U.S. troops land on Leyte. The Pacific Fleet crushes the Japanese in the Battle for Leyte Gulf.

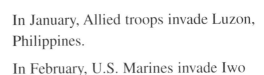
1945

In January, Allied troops invade Luzon, Philippines.

In February, U.S. Marines invade Iwo Jima Island.

In April, U.S. troops land on Okinawa Island.

In August, the U.S. drops an atomic bomb on Hiroshima. Three days later, the U.S. drops an atomic bomb on Nagasaki.

Japan wants peace talks to begin.

Japan accepts surrender terms on August 14, 1945. World War II ends.

The Navajo Code

In 1942, Philip Johnston read an interesting newspaper story. The U.S. military was searching for new codes. They needed words to use on their battlefield radios. One army unit was experimenting with Indian languages.

Johnston jumped to his feet. He had a good idea. And it was time to share it. A week later, he walked into the U.S. Marine office. That was at Camp Elliot in San Diego, California.

He explained that he was not a Native American. But he had grown up on a Navajo reservation. His parents had been Protestant missionaries. As a child, he had learned the difficult Navajo language. Now he was one of the few whites in the country who could speak it.

"Navajo is the language you're looking for," he told the Marines. "You'll have a code no one can break."

Germans had come to the United States in the 1930s to study Indian languages. But Navajo was not one of them. It was a spoken language. It had no written form. So there were no books from which an enemy could learn Navajo.

The Navajo tribe was the largest Indian nation in the United States. Johnston hoped to find plenty of Navajo volunteers. They would have to speak both Navajo and English.

The officers in San Diego liked the idea. But they weren't so sure it would work. They had tried a similar plan during World War I. They had used soldiers of the Choctaw tribe as radio operators.

"We tried the plan for only for a short time," they told Johnston. "It worked quite well. But the Choctaw language did not have words for many military terms."

This would be a problem with the Navajo language too. But Philip Johnston did not give up. He and the Navajos would simply invent new words where they were needed.

"Just let me try," he said. "You'll see how well it can work."

A date was set for a test. Johnston took four Navajos to Camp Elliott. He put them in separate rooms. The men began talking by radio. They translated messages from English to Navajo—then back to English.

The Marine officers couldn't believe it. This Native American code system was faster than anything they'd been using. They had Johnston set up a training program for 30 men.

The Navajo Tribal Council liked the idea. They sent out a call for volunteers. Soon, long lines of young men arrived to apply.

Reservation life had prepared the 30 chosen men for their basic training in the Marines. They easily fit into a program of hard work in the hot, dusty desert. And they knew how to make their canteens of water last. They simply cut the tops off prickly pear cactus plants. Then they sucked out the liquid.

After basic training, the Navajo code talkers learned radio transmission. And radio repair. They were taught to lay wire and climb poles.

Then they began their most important chore. They would form a code for 211 military terms. These words had to be simple enough to memorize. There would be no code books that might fall into enemy hands.

Johnston and the Navajos turned to nature for some of their terms—

> A dive-bomber soared down like a sparrow hawk. So
> it was called *gini*.

An observation plane was curious like an owl. So it became a *ne-as-jah.*

A bomb looked like an egg. So it was called *a-ye-shi.*

A submarine was like an iron fish. It was called *besh-lo.*

Finally, the men translated all 211 terms into code. America was called *ne-he-mah,* the Navajo term for "our mother."

The Marines were excited about the new secret code. They put Johnston in charge of training. And they sent two of the 30 trained men back to the reservation to find more volunteers.

More than 400 Navajo code talkers saw action. Some served as radiomen in Europe. Others went to the Pacific. The Japanese were never able to break their code. Over time, new weapons, planes, and ships wented into battle. These men made up 200 more terms.

The Navajos were valuable to the Marines in other ways. They were good at night scouting. And they could carry heavy radio equipment long distances. They also knew how to walk without making a sound. And they could hide out of the enemy's sight.

One special danger awaited the code talkers. Navajos have dark hair, brown skin, and high cheekbones. So they were sometimes mistaken for Japanese soldiers. Several of the men were nearly shot by fellow Americans.

To keep them safe, some troops assigned a bodyguard to each of their Navajo radiomen.

Code talkers served in Europe and in all six Marine Corps divisions in the Pacific. Eleven were killed in action. The rest returned to the reservations after the war. They were happy to see peace at last.

They had served their country, "our mother," well.

Chapter

The Secret City

In 1942, a group of men stood on a hillside. They were from the United States Army Corps of Engineers. They were in eastern Tennessee. Below them was a gentle valley. It was exactly what they had been looking for.

This rough yet beautiful land was at the foot of the Appalachian Mountains. For 100 years, family farms had dotted these hills. Small towns had sprung up here and there. Up in the hills were a few simple cabins. They had no electricity or running water.

Some might have called the area old-fashioned. Indeed, time seemed to have passed it by. But now it was time for a change.

At this point, Hitler's troops were sweeping across Europe. The United States had entered the war. The fighting seemed likely to continue for years. And things were growing worse. The Japanese were coming closer.

But then a letter, with a shocking idea, arrived at the White House. It was a letter from Albert Einstein. He was a famous German scientist. The letter was about the war.

Einstein was famous for his work in physics. Then the Nazis came into power. In 1933, Einstein was visiting England and the United States. The German government seized his property. They also took away his German citizenship.

Now there was no reason for Einstein to go home. So he took a job in the U.S. He became a mathematics professor at Princeton University in New Jersey.

But Albert Einstein knew what scientists were doing in Germany. They were on the verge of an important discovery. All over the world, people wanted to produce atomic power. The Germans were close to the answer. If they found it, Nazi Germany could blow up the entire world.

In his letter to Roosevelt, Einstein said that he, too, was close to the secret of the atom. Would the United States like to have his scientific studies?

There were other fine German scientists who had escaped from the Nazis. "They will help," Einstein said. In addition, the well-known Italian physicist, Enrico Fermi, had promised to work with them.

Roosevelt made a bold decision. He agreed to a secret plan. It would be called "The Manhattan Project." The president didn't dare talk about it with Congress. If he did, there would be too many ways for the secret to get out.

Soon the 59,000 acres in Oak Ridge, Tennessee, had been chosen. It had plenty of water. A nearby dam would provide electricity.

The government was taking over the valley. It needed the valley for the best interests of the American people. This policy is called *eminent domain.*

The few families that lived in the area were offered very good prices for their homes. They had 90 days to move away. Some were very angry. Others believed there was an important reason for them to agree.

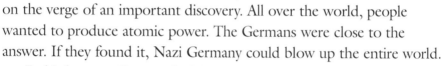

The Manhattan Project needed workers. The builders came first. They lived in 6,000 trailers brought in from all over the eastern U.S. Each group of several trailers was placed in a circle around a central bathhouse.

Separate from the trailers were "hutment" areas. Some were for men. And others were for women. These one-room apartments were 16' by 16'. Each had a wood floor, a thin sheet of plywood for walls, and a potbellied stove.

Months went by. Then the wives and children of the workers moved to the secret city. Now homes, grocery stores, and schools were needed.

Everyone floated in a sea of mud that first year. For weeks, record-breaking rains fell.

Prefabricated, or already built, houses were brought to Oak Ridge in sections. They went up right away for the top scientists. The houses arrived complete with plumbing, electric lines, furniture, and curtains.

The rains continued. And mud oozed around the doorways. Construction workers labored 70 hours a week. They had no time to bother with porches, paths, and driveways.

Also prefabricated were the military quarters for the special engineering staff. These 98 dormitories housed 140 or 540 soldiers apiece.

The construction was finally completed. And a total of 8,700 buildings served a population of 75,000.

Life went on for the residents of the secret city. There were a few simple theaters. (Those served as churches too.) Food choices were limited.

Large grocery chains that received orders from the area would look at the map. There was no city listed. So they saw no reason to ship so much food to a handful of rural residents! The suppliers had to keep in mind that supplies were scarce. So they cut the food and drug orders. This meant long, tedious lines in the Oak Ridge mud.

For the children, growing up in a secret city was not much fun.

The government warned families not to leave town. They asked the people of Oak Ridge to stay behind the fences. Every visit to the outside could result in a slip of the tongue.

Having visitors come in was even more difficult. Besides, gasoline was rationed. So few people in the U.S. traveled outside their own towns. Sadly, the residents had to keep to themselves. They went without family reunions. And they gathered with just their neighbors for holidays.

Oak Ridge had a large Girl Scout troop. Members signed up at national headquarters without addresses or last names. This was the only time in the history of the organization that this happened. For all ages at Oak Ridge, social life was restricted. People could only associate with friends and neighbors within the project's fence.

There were three buildings filled with science labs. These were

purposely located in different parts of the valley. Each worker knew only his own job. He was but a small part of the Manhattan Project. Only Einstein, Fermi, and five other scientists knew how the jobs at the three sites worked together.

President Roosevelt died in April 1945. The new president, Harry Truman, knew nothing of the Manhattan Project until he became president. It was his job to decide how to use the work at Oak Ridge.

The U.S. dropped atomic bombs on Hiroshima and Nagasaki. At last, the people of Oak Ridge could know the whole story of their secret city. They had all been working to find how atomic power could be used.

Many had family members fighting in the Pacific. Perhaps the work at Oak Ridge had kept those men and women alive. For thousands would have died in an invasion of the Japanese islands.

Fortunately, the war ended instead. Now scientists could turn to peaceful uses for the atomic products of Oak Ridge, Tennessee. And the fences could come down forever.

Chapter 13

Peace Returns

World War II took more lives than any other war in history. It destroyed whole cities. It left nations with huge debts. Rubble filled the streets of Europe and Asia. Thousands of people had no homes. It would take many years to rebuild.

It was April 1945. A conference of 50 countries met in San Francisco, California. They drew up plans for the United Nations. That organization helps maintain world peace. More than 50 years later, the United Nations is still going strong. It serves as a place where nations try to settle their problems peacefully.

On the U.S. mainland, the end of war meant happier times. Servicemen and servicewomen came home. Families were reunited. And, largely because of the war effort, the Depression was over.

Nancy and Bob were glad to see the war end. Bob, now 19, had been drafted at 18. Their father had enlisted for Navy duty. He would soon be home.

Rationing ended. Markets had full shelves again. Clothing items like shoes and stockings were in the stores. The family could take a drive without worrying about how much gas it took. And now, new cars would be built again.

Perhaps best of all, the government had passed the G.I. Bill of Rights. Bob, as a returning serviceman, could use the G.I. Bill. If he decided to go to college, the government would pay most of his fees. Young men whose families had never had money for college could look forward to earning a diploma.

Builders put up small homes. Row after row and street after street, these *tract houses* became the new look of America.

The government made home ownership possible. A new tract home sold for about $8,000. Through the G.I. Bill, a family could take out a low-interest loan. And they could live in one of those homes for $60 a month.

Most new tract houses were in the suburbs. Many women who had worked in factories during the war were happy to quit. A new house was their dream. It would be the best place to raise a family.

A free America, recovering from the horrors of war, moved forward.

Glossary

aerial   from the air

ally   a state, country, or person who associates or joins forces with another by mutual agreement

barge   a flat-bottomed boat used for the transport of supplies

barracks   housing for soldiers

chancellor   the chief minister of state in some European countries

convent   a place where Catholic nuns live

death camp   someplace Jews and others were forced to go to be killed by the Nazis during World War II. They were also known as *extermination* camps. Other Jews were taken to work camps and concentration camps.

depth charges	a weapon used against submarines. They are like drums filled with explosives that are dropped into the sea. Also called a depth bomb.
dictator	a person who has absolute power to rule a country
drafted	to have been selected for—and be obligated to—military service
hangar	a shelter in which aircraft are housed and repaired
invade	to enter for conquest
latrine	a hole dug in the earth for use as a toilet
paratrooper	a soldier who is trained and equipped to parachute from an airplane
pontoon	a float of a seaplane
reconnaissance	an inspection or exploration of an area to gain military information about the enemy
satellite	an object that is built specifically to orbit the earth
shell	ammunition that carries an explosive charge
suburb	a smaller community on the outskirts of a city
surrender	to give up; to admit defeat
telegraph	a device that enables communication at a distance. Coded signals are electrically transmitted over wires.

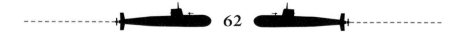

Index